30 Ways

To Advertise Your Business To

Get New Customers

Increase

SALES & PATRONAGE

(For New Business Owners)

Agnes Fidelis

Disclaimer

.The mention of specific platforms in this book does not imply endorsement or recommendation by the author. The information provided is based on the author's experiences and research and is not intended to replace professional advice.

Every effort has been made to accurately represent information in this book at the time of publication.

It is recommended to consult with a qualified professional before making any decisions based on the information provided in this book.

By reading this book, you agree to the terms of this disclaimer and recognize that the author and publisher are not responsible for the success or failure of your actions relating to the information presented herein.

Introduction

Importance of Advertising and Marketing to the Growth and sustainability of any business

Advertising and marketing are important factors of a company's growth and sustainability. They enable business possessors to engage with guests.

Advertising and marketing contribute to the success of a business.

Below are some Important reasons why you should Advertise your business :

1. Visibility and Brand Awareness:

2. Customer Acquisition:.

3. Market Differentiation:

4. Product and Service Promotion:

5. Customer Loyalty and Retention:

6. Revenue Generation:

7. Market Adaptability:

8. Online Presence and Digital Engagement:

9. Data-Driven Decision Making:

10. Crisis Management and Reputation:

11. Employee Morale and Recruitment:

12. Global Reach:

13. Adaptation to Technological Changes:

Chapter One

Online Platforms/Ways/Channels To

Advertise Your Business

1. Social Media Platforms:

• Facebook :

- Is one of the widely-used platform for business promotion

- You can create your business presence on Facebook Platform

- The Platform also gives you the opportunity to Advertise your business to new customers, and engage with your existing customers.

- Showcasing your business on this platform could help you acquire new clients.

• Instagram :

- is one of the best platforms for visual content

- Instagram is effective for businesses with a strong visual appeal

- Advertising on the Instagram platform can help you earn new potential customers for your business.

• **Twitter** :

- is one of the platforms where people go to get real-time updates

- Twitter is suitable for quick engagement

- Showcasing your business on this platform will help you engage with potential prospects who will end up patronizing you.

• **LinkedIn**:

- LinkedIn is a platform for professional networking

- It is ideal for Business To Business marketing

- If your potential prospects are professionals, LinkedIn is one of the best platforms to showcase your business to potential audiences who will patronize your brand.

- **Pinterest** :

- Is one of the visual discovery platform

- Great for businesses with visually appealing products

- This is one of the best platform you can use to showcase your brand and earn some new clients.

• Snapchat :

- If young people are your target audience (that is, people that will need your business), this is one of the best platforms to showcase your brand or business to earn new customers.

- This platform is particularly popular among younger people.

• TikTok:

- Is young people's platform

- If your business is for young people, this is also a good platform to showcase your business.

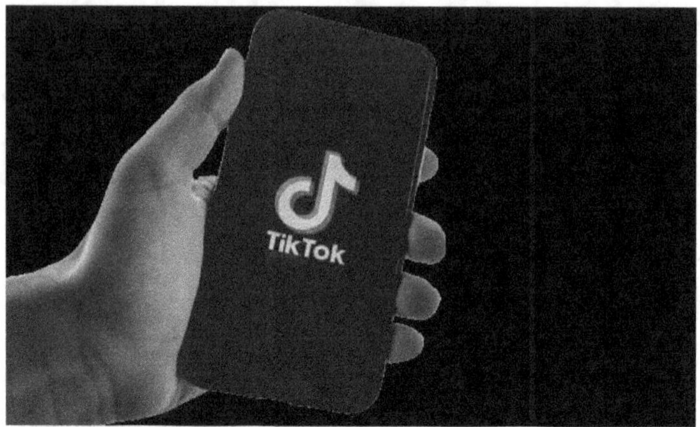

2. Search Engines:

• Google Ads :

- Pay-per-click advertising on Google allows businesses to display advertisements in search results.

- This is an excellent platform to also display your business. As you also know, a lot of people go on Google to search for things.

- it is an opportunity to have your business presence on the platform as well, so that when people search for brands in your niche, your brand will also be visible for them to see.

• Bing Ads :

- This is also similar to Google Ads but targeting the Bing search engine.

- **Yahoo Advertising** :

-This is when you pay Yahoo to help you advertise your business on the Yahoo platform.

- It is also an excellent platform where you can advertise your business to a lot of potential prospects.

3. Content Marketing Platforms:

- **Medium** :

- A platform for long-form content

- Where businesses can share articles and stories.

- **LinkedIn Articles** : This is when you publish articles directly on your LinkedIn profile to showcase expertise.

- **Blogging platforms (WordPress, Blogger)**

4. Video Platforms:

- **YouTube** :

- This is when you pay Yahoo to help you advertise your business on the Yahoo platform.

- It is also an excellent platform where you can advertise your business to a lot of potential prospects.

• **Vimeo** :

- This platform is known for high-quality video content and is often used by businesses for a more professional presentation.

• **IGTV (Instagram)** :

- Instagram's long-form video platform,

- The Platform is also suitable for mobile-centric content.

5. Email Marketing:

• **Mailchimp** :

- It is an email marketing platform

- Businesses use the platform to create and send newsletters and promotional emails.

• **Constant Contact** :

- Another popular platform for email marketing and online surveys.

• **Sendinblue** :

- It is an email marketing and automation platform with a focus on simplicity and affordability.

6. Online Communities:

• **Reddit** :

- It is an email marketing and automation platform with a focus on simplicity and affordability.

• **Quora** :

- It a platform for Question & Answer, where businesses can showcase expertise by answering niche-related questions.

• Online forums related to your industry

7. Podcasting Platforms:

• **Apple Podcasts** :

- Is a major podcast directory and platform for reaching a wide audience.

• **Spotify** :

- Is a popular music and podcast streaming platform where people that are in the music niche can use to promote their music.

• **Google Podcasts** : Google's podcast platform for Android users. It is also a platform which you can use to promote your business.

8. Review and Recommendation Platforms:

• **Yelp** : It is a platform for customer reviews and business ratings.

• **Google My Business** : This platform allows businesses to manage their online presence, including reviews and location information.

• **Trustpilot** : This platform is used for collecting and showcasing customer reviews.

9. Affiliate Marketing Platforms:

• **Amazon Associates**: An affiliate marketing program where businesses can earn commissions for promoting Amazon products. This is also a good avenue to promote your business.

• **ShareASale**: An affiliate marketing network connecting businesses with affiliates.

• **CJ Affiliate** : A global affiliate marketing network.

10. E-commerce Platforms:

• **Shopify**:

- Is an e-commerce platform

- It allows businesses to create online stores.

• **Etsy**:

- Is a marketplace for handmade and vintage goods.

• **Amazon Seller**:

- This platform enables businesses to sell products directly on the Amazon platform.

Chapter Two
Offline Platforms/Ways/Channels To Advertise Your Business

1. Print Media:

• Newspapers:

-Traditional print advertising in local or national newspapers is also a good medium to advertise or promote your business.

• **Magazines**:

- Advertising in industry-specific or general-interest magazines.

• **Brochures**:

- Printed promotional materials providing detailed information about a business or product.

• **Flyers:**

- Single-page promotional materials often distributed in local areas.

2. Television Advertising:

• **Local TV stations** :

- Advertise on local television channels also help businesses to reach a broad audience.

• Cable networks:

- Advertise on specific cable channels based on your target audience is also an ideal way to promote your business.

3. Radio Advertising:

• Local radio stations:

- Run audio adverts on local radio stations to reach a local audience.

4. Direct Mail:

• Postcards :

- Direct mail marketing using visually appealing postcards.

• Catalogs:

- Printed materials showcasing a range of products.

• Letters:

- Personalized direct mail letters to targeted audiences.

5. Outdoor Advertising:

• Billboards:

- Large outdoor advertising displays in high-traffic areas.

- **Buses and transit ads**:

- Advertise on public transportation vehicles or stations.

- **Posters**:

- Display posters in public spaces for local visibility.

6. Event Sponsorship:

- **Sponsor local events or community activities** :

- Support community events or sports teams for brand visibility.

7. Trade Shows and Exhibitions:

- **Participate in industry-specific trade shows**:

- Showcase products or services to a targeted audience.

8. Community Bulletin Boards:

- **Place flyers in local community centers, libraries, and coffee shops**:

- Utilize community bulletin boards for local visibility.

9. Vehicle Advertising:

• **Use vehicle wraps or decals**:

- Advertise on company vehicles for mobile visibility.

10. Networking Events:

• **Attend local business networking events**:

- Build relationships with other businesses and potential clients.

11. Word of Mouth:

• **Encourage satisfied customers to refer your business**:

- Leverage positive customer experiences for referrals.

12. Branded Merchandise:

• T-shirts, hats, pens, etc., with your logo:

- Distribute branded merchandise for brand recognition.

13. Guerrilla Marketing:

• Unconventional and creative methods to promote your business in public spaces:

- Innovative and attention-grabbing marketing tactics.

14. Cold Calling:

• Reach out to potential clients via phone calls:

-Directly contact potential clients to introduce your services.

15. SMS Marketing:

• Send promotions and updates via text messages:

- Engage with customers through text messaging.

16. Community Sponsorship:

• Sponsor local sports teams or community projects: Support local initiatives for community engagement.

17. Loyalty Programs:

• Offer rewards to repeat customers: Encourage customer loyalty through reward programs.

18. Door-to-Door Marketing:

• Distribute promotional materials directly to residences: Target local neighborhoods with physical marketing materials.

19. Chamber of Commerce:

• Join and participate in local chamber events : Engage with local businesses through chamber of commerce events.

20. Public Speaking:

• Offer to speak at local events or workshops: Showcase your expertise by speaking at relevant events.

Remember to evaluate the relevance and effectiveness of each channel based on your business goals, target audience, and budget.

It's often beneficial or important to use a combination of online and offline strategies for a well-rounded marketing approach.

Now that you know these platform, I advise that you take full advantage of them by quickly jumping on any, and showcase your business and start acquiring new customers, get more sale and patronage for your business.

I wish you the best as you embark on your journey...

Cheers.....